FIRST 15 LESSONS

FINGERSTYLE GUITAR

by Chris Woods

Includes Audio & Video Access

T0081874

ISBN 978-1-5400-5231-5

PLAYBACK+
Speed • Pitch • Balance • Loop

To access audio, video, and extra content visit:
www.halleonard.com/mylibrary

Enter Code
4186-2461-0822-7661

7777 W. BLUEMOUND RD. P.O. BOX 13819 MILWAUKEE, WI 53213

Visit Hal Leonard Online at
www.halleonard.com

GUITAR TAB

Throughout this book we will be using guitar tablature, also known as *tab*. This system uses numbers to depict the frets and lines to show the strings. The six lines run from the low E string at the bottom to the high E string at the top. We will be attaching note values to each fret number to help bring the tab to life. Here's a sample:

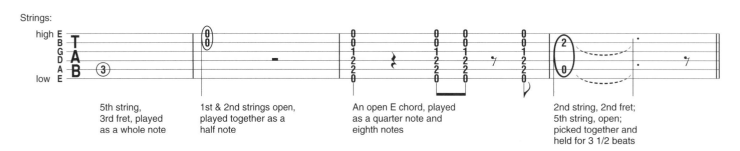

Here's a quick explanation of the note values used in this book:

One *whole note* lasts for four beats. One *half note* lasts for two beats. In 4/4 time, each measure contains four beats and may contain up to one whole note or two half notes. When you see 4/4 at the beginning of a tune, it means that there are four beats per measure, and the quarter note equals one beat. 4/4 is an example of a *time signature*. We'll also look at 3/4 and 6/8 time signatures in later lessons.

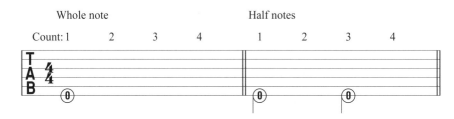

One *quarter note* lasts for one beat. One eighth note lasts for half of one beat. In 4/4 time, each measure may contain up to four quarter notes or eight eighth notes.

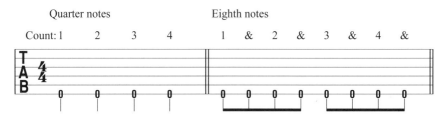

One sixteenth note lasts for a quarter of one beat. In 4/4 time, each measure may contain up to sixteen sixteenth notes.

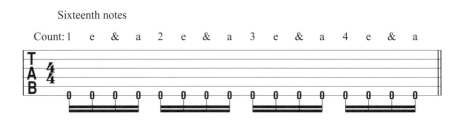

There are many ways to approach fingerstyle guitar playing or fingerpicking. Different guitarists follow different systems, using certain fingers to play certain strings. Some players pick with the thumb and three fingers. Others might only use the thumb and two fingers.

INTRODUCTION TO "PIMA"

The lessons in this book will be working with the most common fingerpicking system, often referred to as "PIMA," which is a really economical way to fingerpick and won't create any limitations down the line. It uses the thumb (p), index (i), middle (m), and ring finger (a). The thumb tends to control the lower strings (low E, A, and D). Usually, the index finger covers the G string, middle finger the B string, and ring finger the high E string. While this is probably the most efficient way to fingerpick, you can still enjoy this book just as much if you approach things differently.

This is your first exercise. We will be picking a simple pattern: down with your thumb (p), and up with the fingers (i, m, or a).

We will be holding an E minor chord with our fretting hand, playing four even quarter notes in each bar. Notice the p, i, m, or a below each note. This helps you understand which finger (or the thumb) in your picking hand to use.

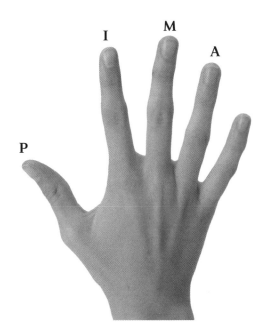

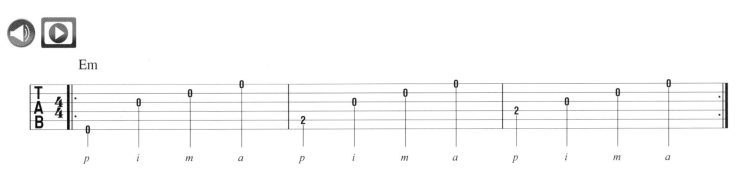

As with almost every example in this book, the first exercise is designed to be played in a loop. The symbols at the beginning and end (||: :||) are known as *repeat signs*. They tell you to go back and play all of the music enclosed within them once more. So, when you reach the end, go back to the start. Each time around, experiment with how strongly you play each note, focusing on keeping your wrist as relaxed as possible.

A NOTE ON FINGERNAILS

You can fingerpick with just the pads of your fingers, with short nails, or—like many guitarists—with longer nails on your picking hand. If you want to try playing with longer nails, you will need to use a fine-grit nail file to file your nails regularly. This will create a smooth surface and keep them at a comfortable length. Nail length and shape is something that differs from player to player, so experiment and see what works for you.

ASCENDING PATTERN WITH OPEN AND FRETTED NOTES

A lot of the fingerpicking you hear in popular music is built around chords. However, using a single fretted note can be enough to bring things to life. This simple *ascending* (moving up in pitch) pattern is a great way to start things. Try this example to get you going. Let each note ring out, experiment with when you move your fretted note, and remember it's designed to be played in a loop—so enjoy playing it around and around.

This is also the perfect time to focus on playing the notes evenly in time and in volume with your picking hand. Paying close attention now will really pay off later. Which finger to use in your picking hand is noted below the tab as *p*, *i*, *m*, or *a*. When you see right-hand fingerings drop out of a tune, that simply means to continue using the same pattern until directed otherwise.

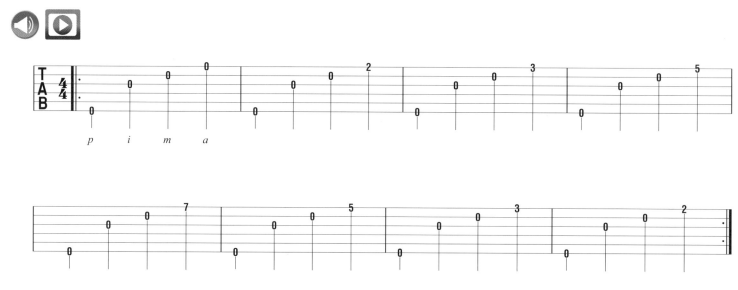

ASCENDING AND DESCENDING PATTERN

Of course, we don't just have to pick in an ascending pattern. We can vary things by *descending* (moving down in pitch) too. This example is an opportunity to blend both ascending and descending patterns. Pay attention to which fingers we use... is it the index finger? Is it the middle finger?

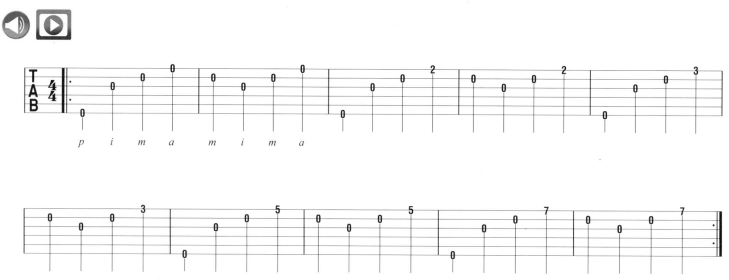

THUMB AND FINGER TOGETHER

The simplest changes can help your playing take a massive leap. In this example, we add the idea of playing two notes simultaneously, using your thumb and one finger together.

In the first bar, we pick the low and high E strings together on the first beat, using the thumb and ring finger. In the second bar, we begin by using the thumb and middle finger together, playing the low E string and the B string. Notice the pattern is the same as the previous example, but with a few added notes.

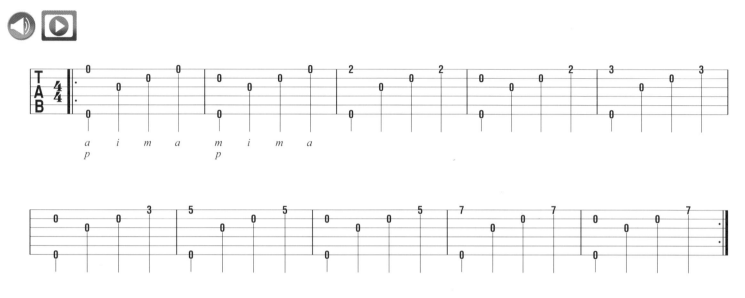

Once you are comfortable with each of these three exercises, it's a good time to start experimenting and creating your own patterns. Notice how each exercise in this lesson uses the same fretted notes on the high E string, with the melody moving from the open string to frets 2, 3, 5, and 7. Try creating your own pattern in your picking hand using these same notes. Strings could be played in a different order to form a different pattern, or you could use your thumb and finger together on different strings.

Try this short exercise to help you get used to playing with your thumb and one finger together on different strings. Then, it's over to you to start creating—but remember to stick to a consistent pattern each time.

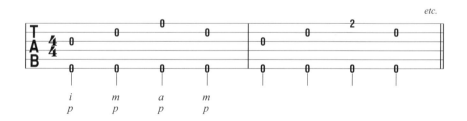

LESSON 3

FINGERPICKING OPEN CHORDS

Fingerpicking the notes of a chord in succession, or playing an *arpeggio*, is probably the most familiar fingerpicking sound. Throughout this lesson, we will only be using the basic open G, C, and D chords. This first exercise is spread across eight measures. The chord sequence remains the same throughout, but the second time through the picking hand switches from a *p-m-i-m* pattern to a *p-i-m-i* pattern. Notice how each bar starts with two notes played together, and the lowest note of the chord, or *root note*, is included in the pair.

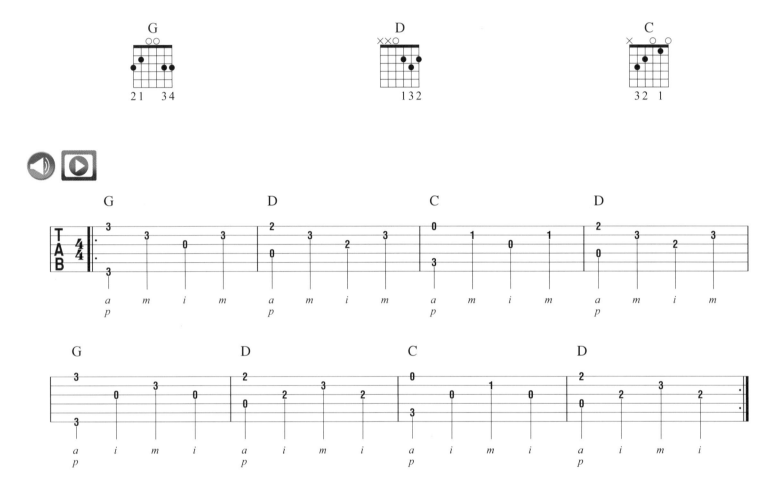

Reading the music for fingerpicking can be a little tricky at times. It is helpful to pay close attention to the chord that is noted above the music, as quite often your fretting hand is simply holding down a chord, and most of the work is done with your picking hand.

Try this simplified classic tune. You'll notice we are using eighth notes now. We will talk about eighth notes more in our next lesson, but for now just enjoy squeezing a few more notes into the bars. Each chord change begins with the root note of the chord shown above the tab.

"The First Cut Is the Deepest"

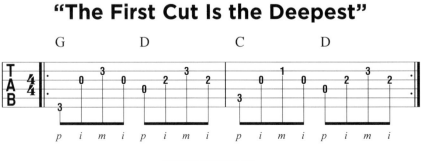

ALTERNATING BASS NOTES

A chord often contains all the notes we need. The simple act of changing the lowest note played by the thumb on the right hand, while keeping the rest of our picking pattern the same, can be enough to make things sound great. In this example, we continue to use the same right-hand pattern for the *i*, *m*, and *a* fingers, but simply alter which string we play with the thumb. In the first measure, we begin by playing the root note of the G chord on the low E string with our thumb. In the second measure, we move away from the root note and start with the thumb on the A string instead. We move the bass note like this for two different chords, G and C.

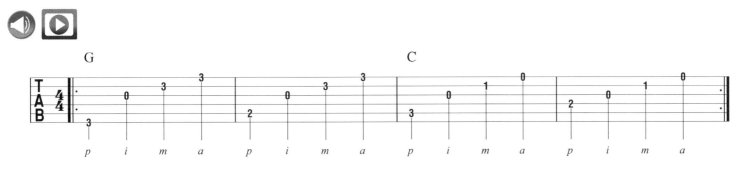

In this exercise, we are starting to mix up playing two notes together, ascending and descending patterns, as well as changing which bass note we play at the start of each bar. Notice how the root note of each chord is still played first.

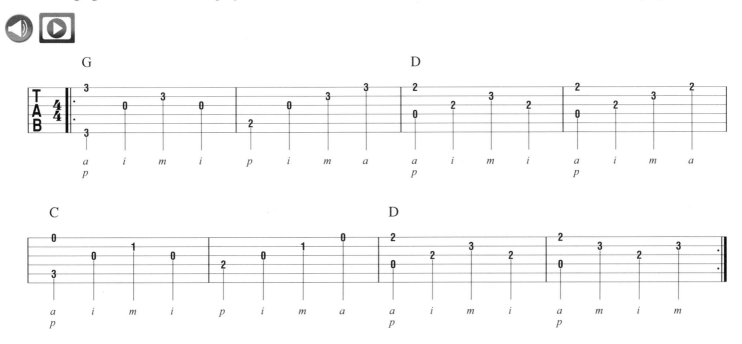

The main riff from the following classic by Radiohead is a great example of a repeated pattern around a simple D chord; however, halfway through the last bar, you break out of the chord and pattern to play four different notes. Use a right-hand fingering pattern that feels most comfortable to you for picking these notes.

"No Surprises"

EIGHTH NOTES

Eighth notes are very common in fingerstyle playing—if you tried playing the popular songs from our last lesson, you would have already used them. To help you in the following example, count "1-&, 2-&, 3-&, 4-&" within each bar, playing a note on both the numbers and the "ands." The numbers are sometimes known as "on beats" and the "ands" are also known as "off beats."

Notice how in this exercise we sometimes use our fingers both on and off the beats, but our thumb is reserved exclusively for "on beats" (or the counted numbers). Keep looping the example, aiming to improve each time.

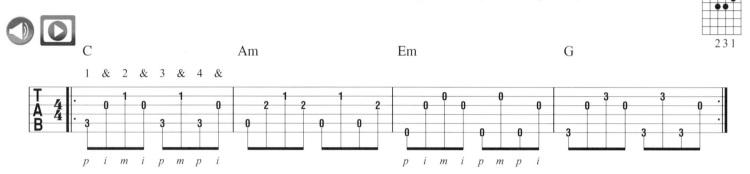

Have a go at playing this classic Clapton track. It uses some simple but great-sounding chords, and crucially our thumb now ends up playing on both the "on beats" and the "off beats." Note: Chords like the Dsus2/F♯ and C/E chords are sometimes referred to as "slash chords." The note name following the slash tells you to use that particular note from the chord as the lowest note in the chord. For example, here we are playing a Dsus2 chord, but using the F♯ from the D chord as the lowest note. Similarly, for the C/E chord, we are simply using a C chord, but using the E from the C chord as the lowest note. You will notice these types of chords throughout the lessons.

"Wonderful Tonight"

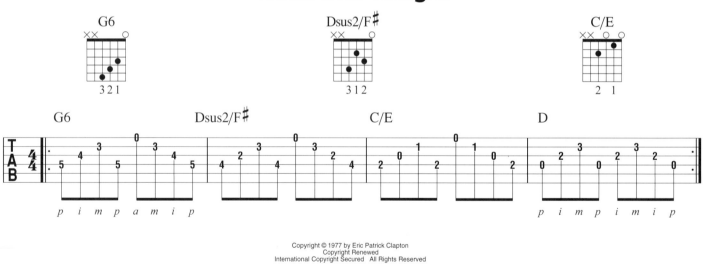

SIXTEENTH NOTES

We are now going to go a step further and squeeze sixteen notes into one measure. You should count, "1-e-&-a, 2-e-&-a, 3-e-&-a, 4-e-&-a." Start as slowly as possible, playing a note on each syllable.

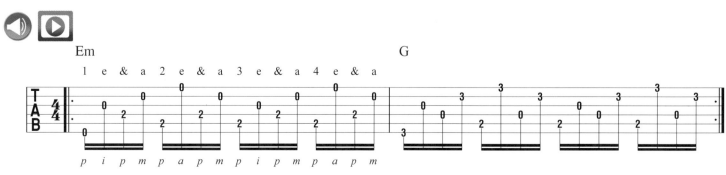

Notice how we are now alternating between the thumb and a finger. This can be really handy when it comes to keeping time—similar to strumming down and up. When you practice this exercise, take your time to feel the momentum between the down of the thumb and the up of a finger. (It will help when we learn about *Travis picking* in the next lesson.)

This simplified extract from Simon and Garfunkel's tune "The Boxer" is a fantastic example of playing sixteen notes in a measure of 4/4 time, and of building up speed bouncing between the down of the thumb and the up of a finger.

"The Boxer"

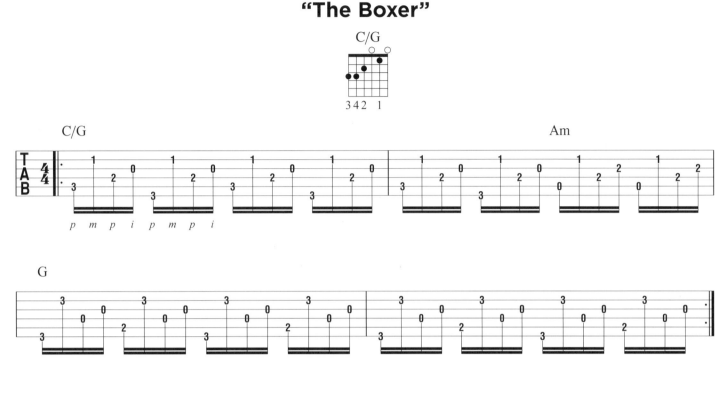

6/8 TIME SIGNATURE

So far, we have only worked with a 4/4 time signature, meaning we have four beats in a measure. While there are plenty of other time signatures out there, 6/8 has to be one of the most popular. One measure of 6/8 may contain up to six eighth notes. Using simple arpeggios, the following example is an opportunity to get a feel for 6/8. Count 1, 2, 3, 4, 5, 6 as you go, playing counts 1 and 4 stronger than the other beats.

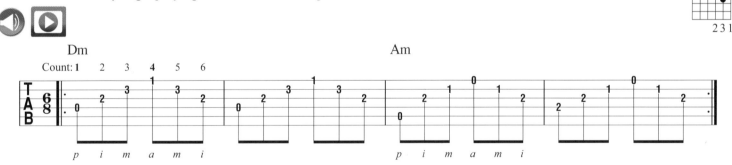

"Everybody Hurts" by R.E.M. is a fantastic example of the hypnotic quality of 6/8.

"Everybody Hurts"

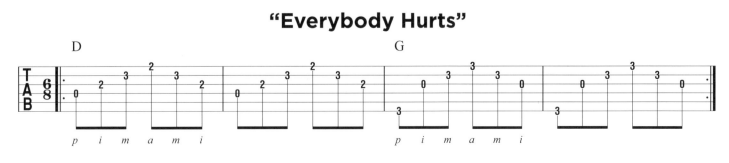

LESSON 5

TRAVIS PICKING

Travis picking is the process of playing a repeated fingerpicking pattern that employs an alternating bass in the thumb (*p*) alongside *syncopated* notes in the fingers (*i, m,* and *a*). It really lends itself to playing eighth-note or sixteenth-note rhythms—we first saw it in the last lesson when looking at sixteenth notes. (We'll talk more about *syncopation* in Lesson 7.) In this famous Taylor Swift song, we use the Travis-picking technique and squeeze a lot of notes into each measure by using sixteenth notes.

"Begin Again"

FINGERS TOGETHER: A PICKED STRUM

In this approach, we are playing with several fingers together at once, picking down with the thumb as normal for the lower bass strings, and then up with three fingers simultaneously.

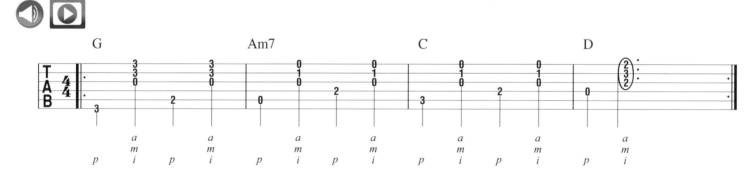

Try playing along with this classic track while picking with several fingers at once.

"Ain't No Sunshine"

VARIATIONS ON THE PICKED STRUM

In this example, we are looking at picking with different combinations of fingers and strings, so rather than always picking up with three fingers, we might pick up with two fingers on the G and B strings, or perhaps on the B and E strings.

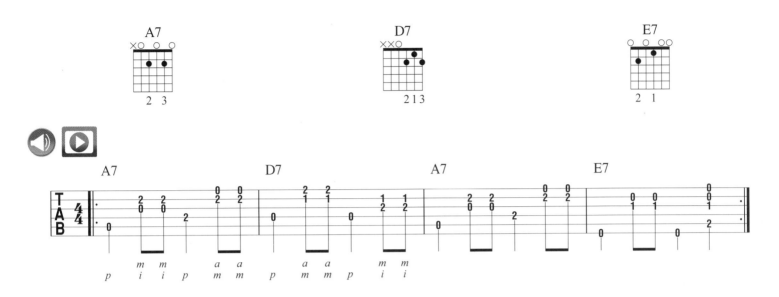

MIXING EIGHTH AND SIXTEENTH NOTES

Mixing eighth and sixteenth notes can create a very cool feel and groove for fingerpicking. Pay attention to where the eighth notes fall and how they mark the beginning of the right-hand pattern.

Eddie Vedder's "Guaranteed" is a great example of the familiar sound of the eighth- and sixteenth-note mix. Try reaching up with your thumb to pick the G string, and using the index finger on the B string and the middle finger on the high E string here for a change.

"Guaranteed"

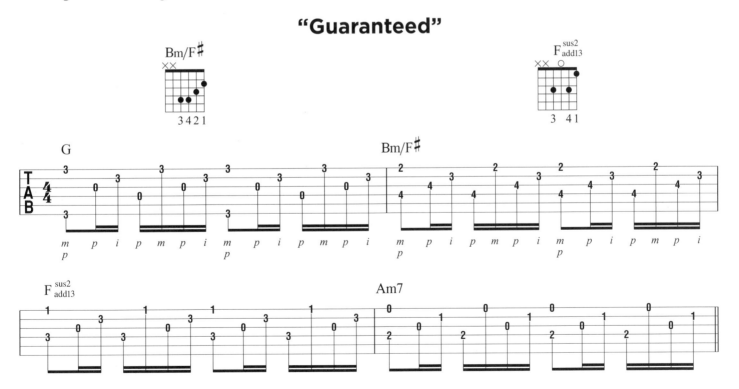

C MAJOR SCALE

Put simply, a *scale* is a collection of notes that sound great together. The chords within a song are also formed from scales; in other words, the notes within scales are the building blocks of songs.

In this lesson, we will be learning the C major scale. Once you know a particular scale, you'll be able to add a handful of those notes into the relevant chord and picking patterns in different ways.

C Major Scale

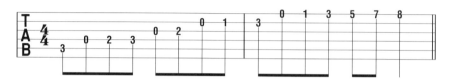

When fingerpicking a chord, we can momentarily add a note from its relevant scale to the existing notes in the chord. This can create a sense of *melody*. It can also help you move smoothly from one chord to the next.

In this example, we are using one additional note from the C major scale (the note G, or fret 3 on the high E string) and momentarily adding it to a C chord and then an A minor chord. Adding just one note to a chord can make a world of difference! While chord names may technically change whenever notes are added, for our purposes in this lesson only the basic chord forms are indicated above the music.

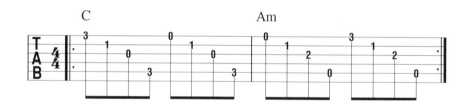

Try this song by the band Kansas. It's a fantastic example of how Travis picking and using extra notes from the scale can work together. Again, only the basic chord forms are indicated above the music.

"Dust in the Wind"

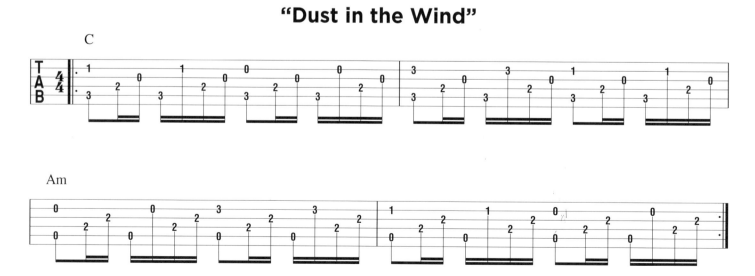

CHANGING BASS NOTES WITHIN CHORDS

When fingerpicking chords, another great way to spice things up is to change a bass note. In previous exercises, we have been playing a different bass note with our picking hand by simply alternating which note our thumb plays within the chord (for example, shifting from the A to D string within a C chord). However, in these examples we will be physically changing the chords' bass notes with our fretting hand, essentially changing the notes within the chord.

The first example is simply working with the humble C chord. The pattern in your picking hand remains the same, but we change the bass note on the A string with our fretting hand. While each bar is technically a different chord, it's best for now to see this as simply making an adjustment to one single chord with your picking hand—a kind of evolution of the chord.

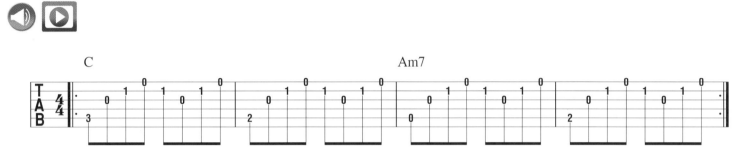

This simple yet effective approach has been used in countless songs in every style. Try out these two song excerpts for inspiration. First, an unexpected track from electronic trip-hop act Massive Attack, which focuses on variations to a simple Dsus2 chord. And finally, the 2001 hit "Wherever You Will Go" by the Calling, which focuses predominantly on a C chord. Note: Throughout the book, it's not necessary to know all the chords presented in parentheses above the music. These are included to help outline the harmonic movement and as inspiration for further study.

"Teardrop"

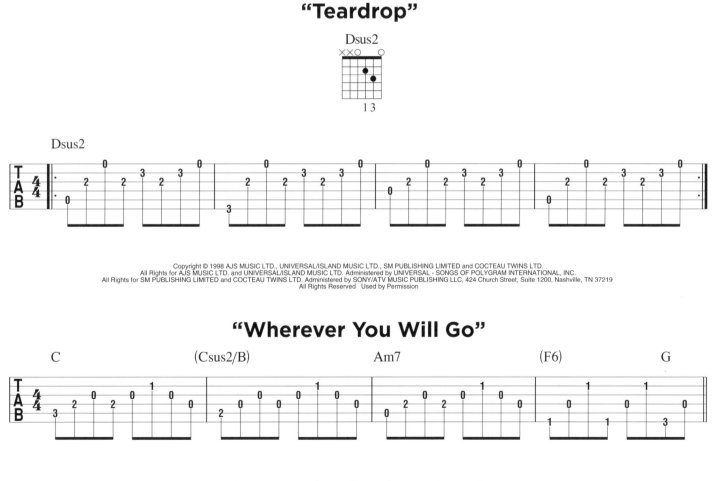

"Wherever You Will Go"

SYNCOPATION

Fingerpicking and fingerstyle music is often at its most exciting when playing *syncopated* rhythms. *Syncopation* occurs when we break from a constant rhythm, often placing emphasis on the "off beats." It is found in virtually all music, and while it can often be a little harder to read, it will sound familiar to you. In this first example, we are picking between two chords. The shorter second bass note and the addition of tied sixteenth notes throughout makes things feel syncopated or "funky."

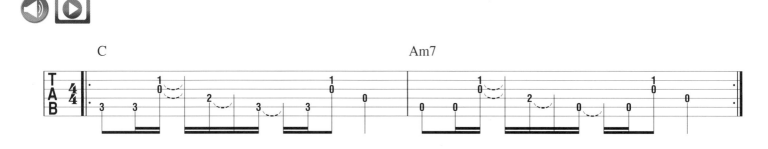

HAMMER-ONS AND PULL-OFFS

We can also introduce more advanced picking-hand techniques into our patterns to bring the syncopation to life. A *hammer-on* refers to the action of playing a note, then snapping a fretting-hand finger down to sound another note without picking again. A *pull-off* uses the same principal but in reverse—we play a fretted note and then pull that finger away, forcing the note to reveal another note by "pulling down" on the string as the finger moves away. Hammer-ons and pull-offs are also often referred to as *slurs*.

Try this very simple example. The first bar contains a hammer-on and the second bar contains a pull-off.

Once you are confident with the previous example, try adding a hammer-on and a pull-off to our earlier syncopated example.

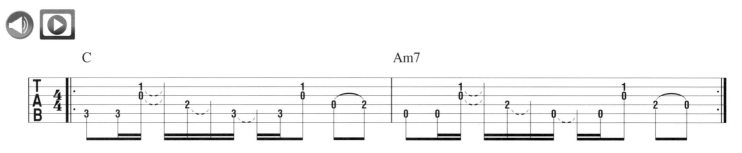

Try this riff from songwriter and guitarist Ben Harper for a great example of simple syncopation and use of a hammer-on.

"Walk Away"

SLIDES

Of course, *sliding* to a note is another fantastic fret-hand technique that can add flavor to your fingerpicking. There are many different ways to approach a *slide*, but to get us going simply try playing a fretted note and then sliding up to another adjacent fret. Pick only the first note, letting the movement and momentum keep the note singing so that we sound two notes but only pick once.

This first example uses a simple one-fret slide and then leads into a familiar C major chord. Try using the third finger of your fretting hand to play fret 2 on the A string, so that you "land" with the correct finger on fret 3 of the A string to easily form a C major chord.

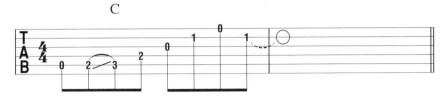

This classic Red Hot Chili Peppers tune brings together hammer-ons and slides brilliantly for some sublime syncopation. Aim for a slow slide joining the two notes on either side of the bar line. Note: In this book, when you don't see a slur above the slide marking, this means to slide between notes but to pick the second note as well.

"I Could Have Lied"

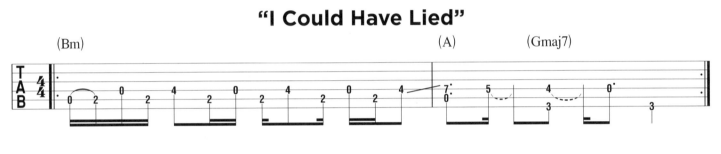

HARMONICS

If you are new to playing *harmonics*, it can take some getting used to. They are achievable on all frets but are simplest on frets 5, 7, and 12... start with 12. Lightly rest a fingertip from your fretting hand on any string directly over the fret wire, without pushing or pressing. Pick the string with your picking hand and move your fretting hand finger away immediately after picking to let the string ring out.

The next example uses harmonics on each string. At the end of the example, with all harmonics "ringing-out," we hammer-on two notes at fret 2 to create an E minor chord. Once this feels comfortable, try the following simplified extract from "Roundabout" by Yes which brings together harmonics, a hammer-on, and a pull-off. Notice that the hammer-on and pull-off come one after the other. You only need to pick the first note in this series.

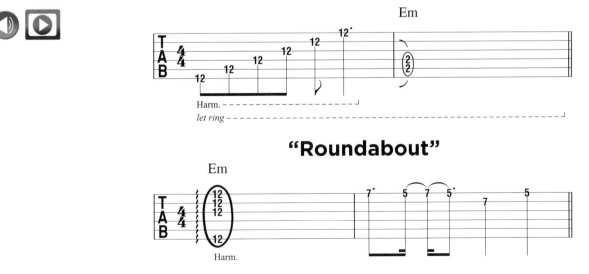

"Roundabout"

This is an iconic fingerpicking track. Don't be put off by the changes from 3/4 to 2/4. A measure of 2/4 contains two beats, while a measure of 3/4 contains three. It's simply a case of having a shorter bar; the "feel" doesn't change at all. Mastering the fourth bar before you move on will really pay off, as the piece is full of repeated picking-hand patterns that relate back to this bar. As we saw in "Guaranteed," it is possible to use a pattern in the measures containing sixteenth notes where the thumb moves up to play the G string in an alternating-bass fashion. The first time you play through the material, take the *first ending*, until you hit the repeat sign four measures later. Then go back and start at the forward-facing repeat sign at measure 3, this time skipping the first ending and continuing on with the *second ending* until you reach the end.

"Blackbird"

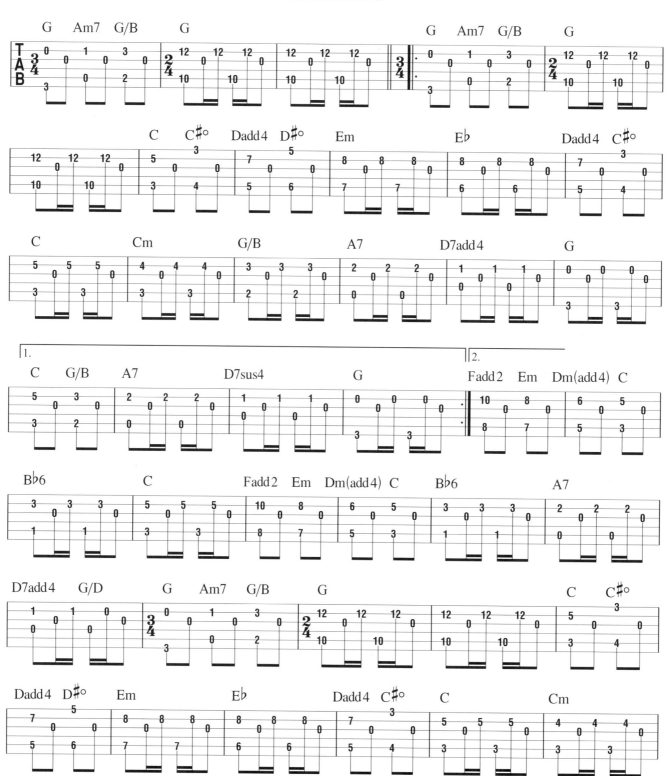

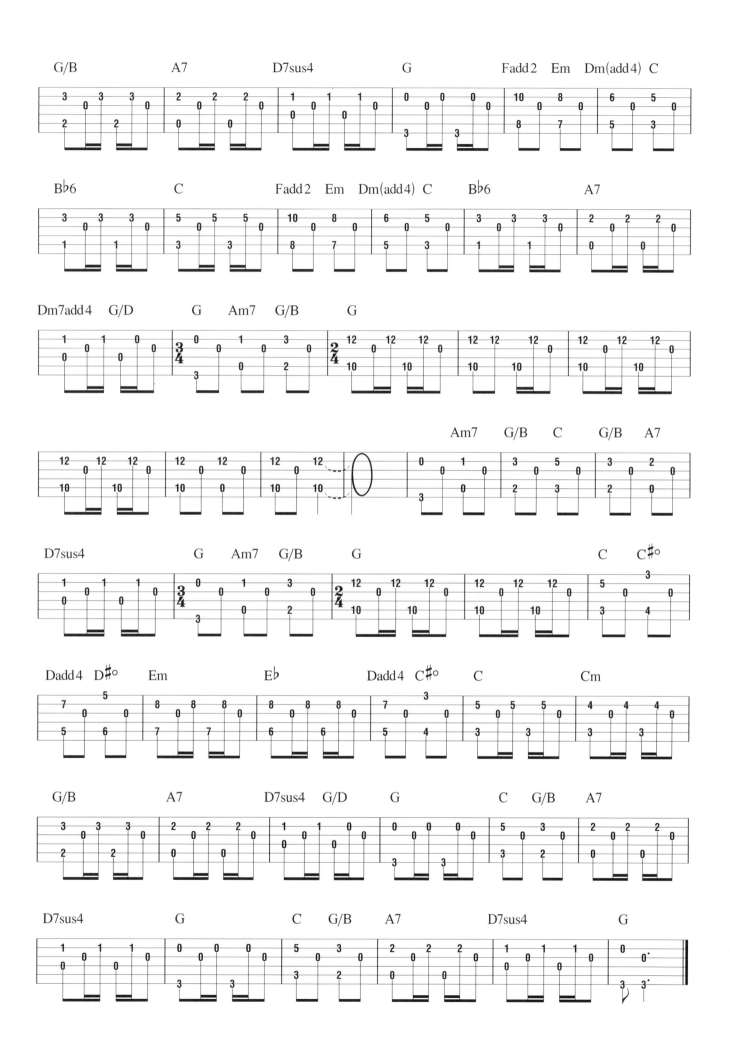

MELODY WITH CHORDS

We have already experimented with adding notes from a scale to a chord in Lesson 6. In this lesson, we are taking that idea to a new level by creating a melody from those notes. We can create melody by adding in notes from a chord's relevant scale, and sometimes even just by choosing notes that are already in the chord. By accenting the chosen melody notes (playing them more loudly), we can make the melody really sing.

In this first example, the first two bars contain a simple melody. The notes are taken from both a basic open C chord and the C major scale. The final two bars bring that melody together with the chords being fingerpicked, using a mixture of melody and arpeggio. The note taken from the C major scale in the final bar will have to be fretted with your little finger, while holding the rest of the chord down as usual. Try picking the melody notes slightly harder to help them stand out from the chord... and remember to play it in a loop.

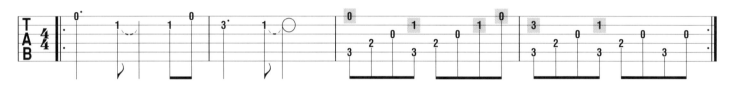

Elizabeth Cotten's "Freight Train" is a fantastic example of mixing arpeggios with melody. The steady arpeggio pattern keeps a hypnotic rhythm while the addition of notes from the C major scale helps to create the melody. It is good to experiment with increasing the volume of the melody notes to help bring out the melody from the rhythmic picking. The alternate G-chord fingering presented here should help you to transition smoothly to the new G7 chord.

"Freight Train"

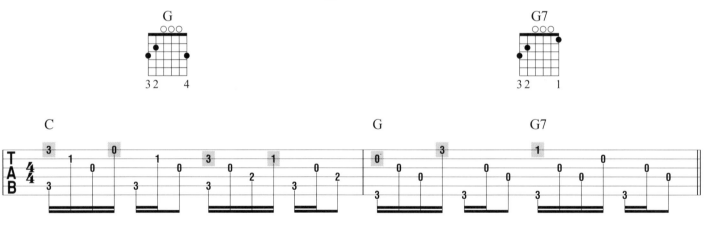

The ability to change volume with each finger will really help bring your fingerpicking to life. In this lesson, it's easy to see how bringing a melody up in volume against arpeggios helps. In other lessons and ways of playing, being able to change volume between fingers will always take your picking to the next level.

MELODY AND HARMONY

When fingerpicking, we don't always have to play our melodies to a backdrop of full chords. We can also take a simple single-line melody and choose a few extra notes to play alongside, creating a fuller sound. This adds *harmony* and can easily be done simply by using notes from the melody's accompanying scale.

In this example, we will be using the scale of E major, building up to playing the emotive and familiar "Amazing Grace."

Play through the following E major scale, enough to feel confident. Try playing it backwards and even starting in different places. It is important to be thinking about your fret-hand fingers and trying to use all of those fingers, as appropriate. As a general guideline, use your first finger for fret 1, second finger for fret 2, third finger for fret 3, and fourth finger for fret 4. (Fret 3 is not used in this scale.)

E Major Scale

Once you are confident with the scale, try playing this arrangement of "Amazing Grace." All of the notes are taken from the E major scale, and several of the notes have a second note played alongside the melody as harmony to create a richer sound.

Notice how you will need to use your index finger in your picking hand to play the D string in the second bar. In this tune, it makes most sense to work with the index, middle, and ring fingers always covering strings D, G, and B respectively, since we never play the high E string. It's not necessary to know the fingering of the full A chord to play this piece, which we'll look at in our next lesson.

"Amazing Grace"

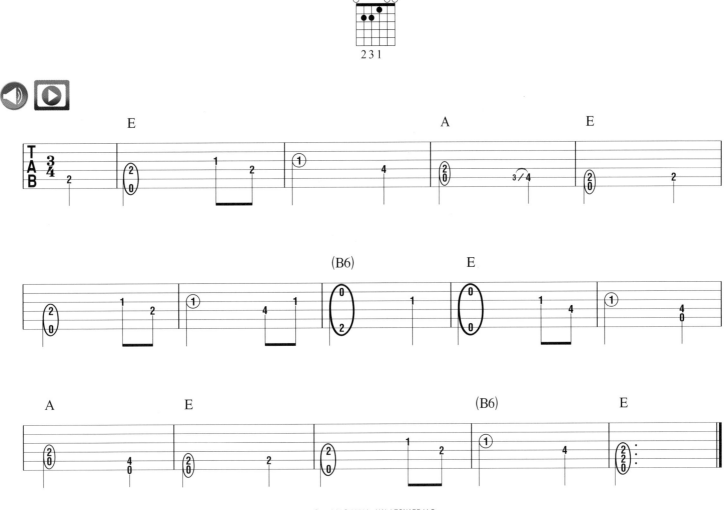

THE GROOVE

Fingerpicking and rhythmic playing go hand in hand. We have already looked at using syncopation and a variety of different "feels" in this book. We can take things a step further by using rests and even percussive sounds, which can really create the sense of a *groove*. A *groove* is, in other words, a repetitive and syncopated rhythm that has space or resting of some kind. In this lesson, we will be focusing on exactly that, creating a groove.

RESTS

Resting is often the key to playing a groove. In this first example, you'll notice a *rest* on the third beat. It is called a *rest* because we literally give the sounds from the guitar a rest, creating silence. Use your fretting hand or your picking hand to stop the strings from vibrating before going on to play the next note. Try playing the notes of the chords with *p*, *i*, and *a* together, and then *i*, *m*, and *a* together. Choose which approach feels more natural to you. There are a few different ways to finger an A chord with the left hand, but you may find the suggested fingering here to be the easiest.

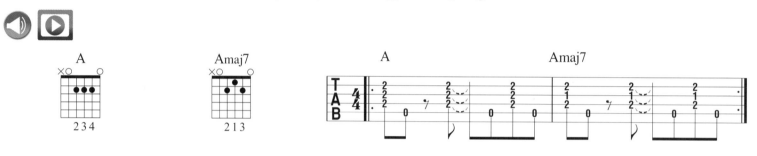

The following track from Eric Clapton's famous *Unplugged* album is an excellent example of a fingerstyle groove played on an acoustic guitar. There are three rests to look out for, so experiment with how you stop the strings from vibrating each time. Choose the one that works best for you in each situation.

"Signe"

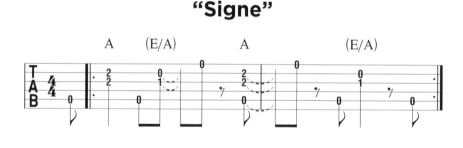

THE STRING SLAP

String percussion is a fantastic element to add to your rhythmic fingerpicking. It is something you may well have naturally done while playing already. To create a *string slap* (which will be notated here with a single "X"), simply turn your picking-hand thumb against the lower strings to create a "click" sound. Imagine you are turning a key in a door—the movement comes from your wrist. The following example blends repetitive basic open chord arpeggios with string slaps on beats two and four, notated as "X."

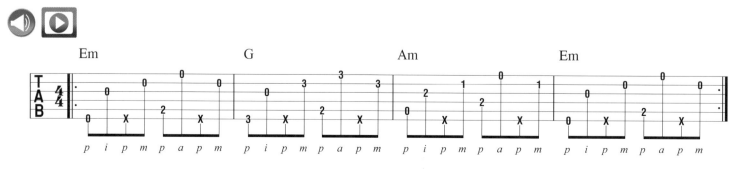

GROOVE AND SLAP

Blending the feel of a groove with a string slap can be quite a natural process since slapping the strings can effortlessly also stop the strings from vibrating, creating a natural rest. This exercise is a copy of the first example from this lesson but with the addition of the string slap, which naturally creates our rest and can be used to prepare your right hand for whatever needs to be played next.

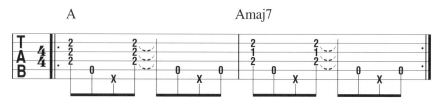

You will find string slapping in a whole host of popular fingerpicked tracks. As with all your picking movements, it is worth experimenting with the volume you can create to give you greater control over your sound. Just as we picked different notes at different volumes in the previous lesson, experiment with how hard (or loudly) you slap the strings. Try the following examples to see how effortlessly this technique may be fit into popular songs.

"Stand by Me"

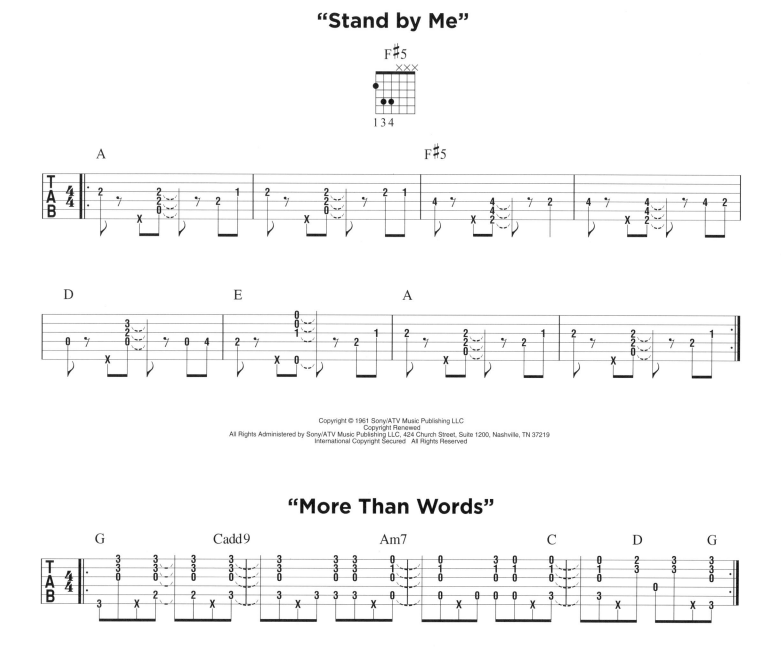

"More Than Words"

THE BLUES SCALE

Whether fingerpicking a blues song or just taking influence from the notes, scales, and chords of the blues, it is (along with jazz) undoubtably a genre every fingerpicker needs to explore. In this first example, we will be getting used to a simple E *blues scale*. Play the scale up and down until you are confident. Once you feel comfortable, experiment with the scale by playing the notes in different orders. Perhaps, try to create a melody. Try harmonizing different notes in the scale with a low open E or open A, calling on some of the ideas from previous lessons.

E Blues Scale

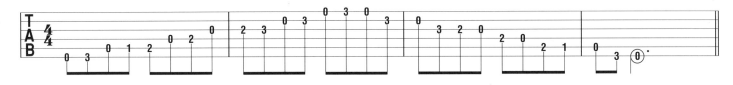

REPEATED-BASS BLUES

In this example, we are looking at playing a handful of notes from the E blues scale to create a melody, complimented with a repeated bass moving from the low E string to the A string. Notice how after almost every note there is a rest helping to create a sense of groove. Approach the rests by touching (stopping) the string with your picking hand fingers immediately after playing. The rests are there as a guide only and there is no need to strictly stick to each rest—you can vary things according to how you feel, phrasing the exercise in a different way each time. You can also try only resting the bass note with your thumb to create a real separation between melody and bass.

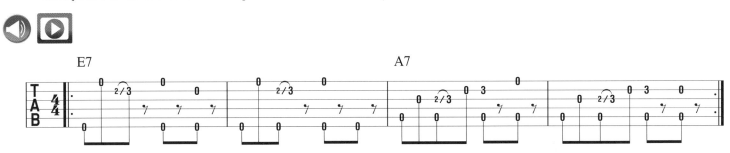

When working though this exercise, it is again well worth your time to focus on the volume of the notes you play. You can experiment with bringing up the volume of the bass notes played with the thumb, and then the same with the melody notes played with the fingers. The benefit of doing this is to give you more control and to make what you do more musical and expressive.

BLUES CHORDS AND 12-BAR BLUES

There is an array of fantastic sounding chords that can go alongside our blues scale or can work all on their own. Try these "bluesy" E13 and A13 chords to get started. Notice how similar they are to the E7 and A7 chords that we already know.

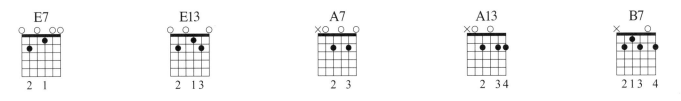

Using these five chords, try this relaxed *12-bar blues*. The following example uses the basic 12-bar blues pattern of four bars of E7 (E7 or E13 in our example), two bars of A7 (A7 or A13 in our example), two bars of E7 (E7 or E13 in our example), finishing with one bar each of B7, A7, E7, and finally B7.

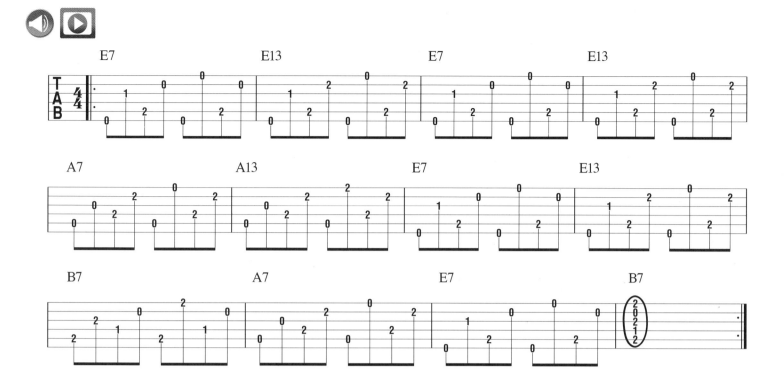

Blues and jazz chords can have fantastically exciting names, but often they are simply familiar chords with another note from the scale added. In blues and jazz, the 13 chord, 7 chord, and most other numbered chords are very common as they all have a fantastic, rich sound.

This short arrangement of the tune "Georgia on My Mind" uses a mix of familiar chords with some more "bluesy" sounding variations too. The new marking above the beginning of the staff tells you to play the tune with a swing feel. Listen to the original to get an idea of how this sounds. Note: A 6 chord adds the same note as a 13 chord, except the added note is played close to the root rather than added to the top of the chord.

"Georgia on My Mind"

UNDERSTANDING HOW BARRE CHORDS WORK

Barre chords use chord shapes that can be moved around the fret board using a flat and straight finger, otherwise known as a barre. Because the strings are covered by the barre and other fingers, the chord keeps its character (major, minor, etc.) and simply changes key. It takes a long time to build up the strength to hold a barre chord, but your first challenge is to understand how they work. Strength will come with time.

In this lesson, we will be looking at barre chords with their root note on the low E string or A string. Look at the shapes presented in the following table. The curved line above the chord grid tells you that your first finger will stretch across several strings at once. Take note of how the barre chord shapes relate to the relevant open chord shapes. (The normal fingerings for the open chords have been adjusted here to demonstrate this more clearly.) Note: For major barre chords on the A string, you may also finger this using the first finger on the root and a third-finger barre across the D, G, and B strings, omitting the highest note of the chord on the high E string. For a good workout, play through the barre chords below in order, following along with the audio or video. Don't worry if this is too difficult at first. With practice it will become much easier.

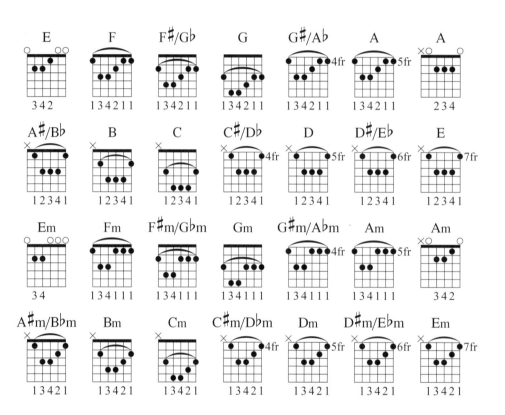

Notice how you can move the "E shape" up a fret, with the barre behind it, and the chord quite literally goes up a note name each time. This is because the shape and relationships remain the same, so the quality of the chord is the same (major, minor, etc.) but the root note changes. For example, an E major chord becomes an F major chord.

USING BARRE CHORDS

In the following example, we are going to use a familiar open E minor chord mixed with barre chords. You should be used to playing G and A minor as open chords, but now we are using a barre chord shape for each. Try your best to hold down each barre chord entirely, even though some of the notes are not sounded in this exercise.

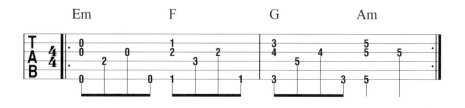

This Jack Johnson track is a great way to get used to barre chords. Aside from being a catchy song, the barre chords are only played for a short part of the time—so your hand gets a chance to rest. The "X's" across all strings in this song refer to a quick, percussive strum across all strings with the right hand while the left hand mutes every string by resting on them lightly without pressing down. Note: "N.C." above the music means "no chord."

"Banana Pancakes"

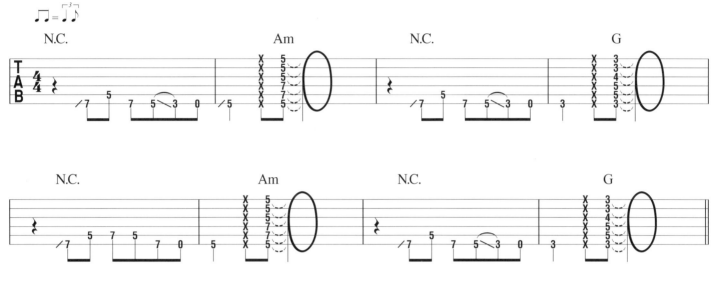

In this example, we are switching between barre chords on the E string and the A string. It shows how learning barre chords on both strings can make things easier for you. For example, notice how the B minor with its root on the A string is much closer to the G barre chord with its root on the sixth string than the B minor with its root on the E string is (which would be played with its root all the way up on fret 7).

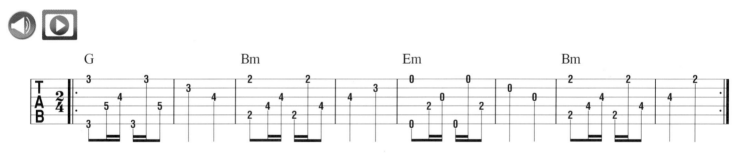

Check out the following song by Green Day for further barre chord adventures.

"Wake Me Up When September Ends"

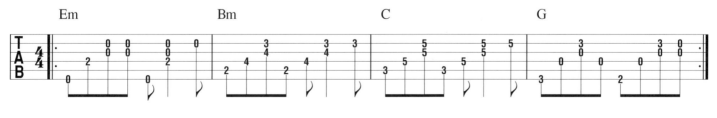

DROP D TUNING

In this lesson, we are going to talk about three different alternate tunings: Drop D, DADGAD, and Open D. The following chart will help you get into each tuning.

	Drop D			**DADGAD**			**Open D**	
D	Low E string	Tune down to D	D	Low E string	Tune down to D	D	Low E string	Tune down to D
A	A string	Leave the same	A	A string	Leave the same	A	A string	Leave the same
D	D string	Leave the same	D	D string	Leave the same	D	D string	Leave the same
G	G string	Leave the same	G	G string	Leave the same	F#	G string	Tune down to F#
B	B string	Leave the same	A	B string	Tune down to A	A	B string	Tune down to A
E	High E string	Leave the same	D	High E string	Tune down to D	D	High E string	Tune down to D

Tuning the strings differently can create a new and exciting sound for you—and new harmonic opportunities for your fingers. In this first example, we are going to simply tune the low E string down to a D. This tuning is known as Drop D tuning.

If doing this by ear, the simplest way to get into this tuning is to play the open D string at the same time as the low E string, and slacken the E string until it vibrates in tune with the D string. Of course, an electronic tuner will make things easier.

Drop D tuning gives us a far "chunkier" sound, while it also makes playing in the key of D much easier. In this example, you will be fretting a D minor chord, but do not fret the high E string at all. Use your index (and pinky) finger to fret the changing bass notes instead. Since we don't play the high E string, it may make sense to have the *i*, *m*, and *a* fingers covering the D, G, and B strings, respectively. The second example below, the intro from "Angelina" by Tommy Emmanuel, is a tricky but rewarding look at using Drop D tuning.

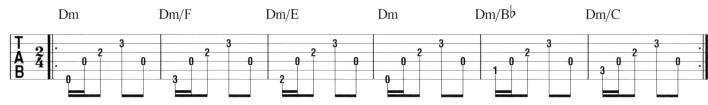

"Angelina"

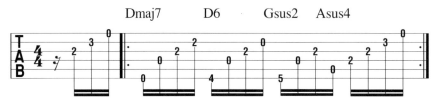

DADGAD TUNING

One of the most popular tunings—especially in the fingerstyle world—is DADGAD tuning. It also gets referred to as the Dsus4 tuning, since the notes make up the chord of Dsus4.

DADGAD tuning is particularly common in Celtic genres of music. This is a short arrangement of the Irish tune "Sheebeg and Sheemore (Si Bheag, Si Mhor)." Notice that there are three beats in each bar and fingers *i*, *m*, and *a* may need to shift between covering strings 4, 3, and 2, and strings 3, 2, and 1.

"Sheebeg and Sheemore (Si Bheag, Si Mhor)"

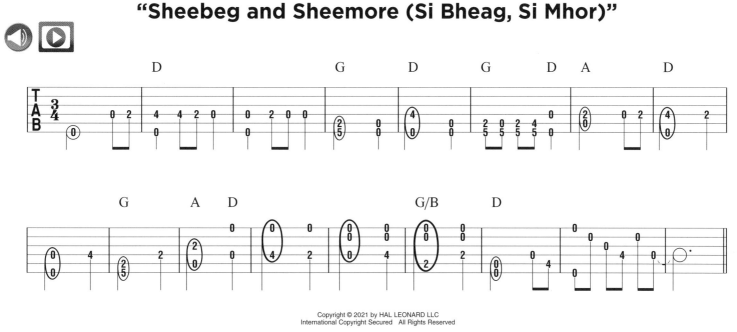

OPEN D TUNING

In Open D tuning, the open strings played together make the sound of a D major chord. Also known as DADF♯AD, Open D tuning is another widely used alternate tuning. If you are already in DADGAD, to get to this tuning you can simply drop your G string down to an F♯. You can use fret 4 on the D string as a reference. As with all tunings, it creates a different sound and opens up new ideas.

This example uses very basic two-finger chord shapes. The shapes aren't related to anything obvious in standard tuning, but you'll find the simplicity creates a new, exciting sound. Try using only one or two fingers to create your own chord shapes in this tuning. Again, you may find that shifting your *i*, *m*, and *a* fingers to cover strings D, G, and B will work best in your picking hand for this example.

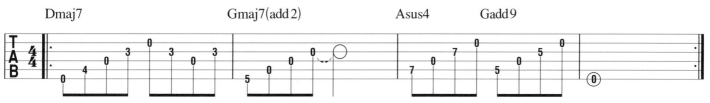

Nick Drake was a pioneer of open (or alternative) tunings, tuning his guitar in exciting ways. He also played some fantastic finger-picking patterns. This tune is in 3/4 time and uses simple two-finger chords.

"One of These Things First"

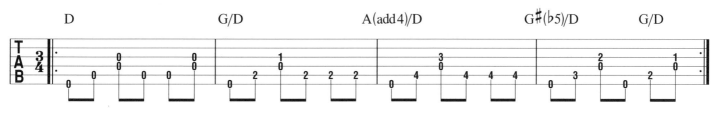

It is great to break up your picking patterns with a *fill*, something that freshens things up. Different techniques can be featured in a fill to ornament your fingerpicking. Back in Lesson 7, we were looking at hammer-ons, pull-offs, slides, and harmonics, all of which can be perfect for using in fills. In this lesson, we'll be looking at those and more.

BENDS

One advanced technique that we haven't looked at until now is the bend. It is a great technique to bring into fingerstyle playing and can really add a vocal element to the gaps between your picking patterns.

Try this first example to get you going with bending. We are playing a *semitone* or half-step bend here, so first fret the note with your second finger, then pluck it and bend the string with your fretting-hand finger so the pitch matches the pitch of the fret above. Take your time to experiment with the timing of the bend. Also, try bending with your third finger, then try using your fourth finger. Adding another finger behind the bending finger on the same string for support may help if you have trouble bending the string all the way.

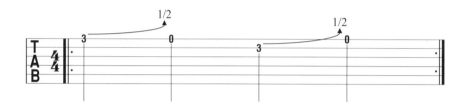

Once you feel confident with the bend, you should try this example which uses a constant picking pattern along with a fill containing a bend. Notice it uses a fantastic version of E7 with the little finger on fret 3 of the B string, moving on and off to create a sense of melody. It is most economical to fret the bends with your little finger. As notated here, the quarter-step bend is a slight bend, not quite reaching the pitch of the fret above.

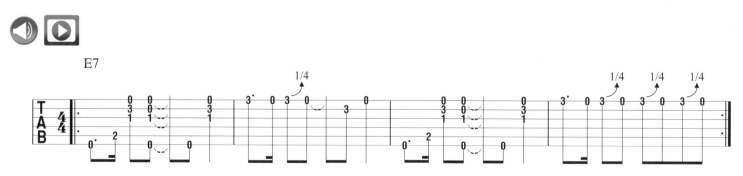

HAMMER-ON AND PULL-OFF FILLS

You are probably nice and familiar with pull-offs and hammer-ons by now. They are great for complimenting syncopation in your picking, but they can also be great to decorate a pattern as a fill.

Try this example (as always play it in a loop) and notice how the hammered-on and pulled-off notes at the end of the phrase, or the fill, fit nicely into an A minor chord.

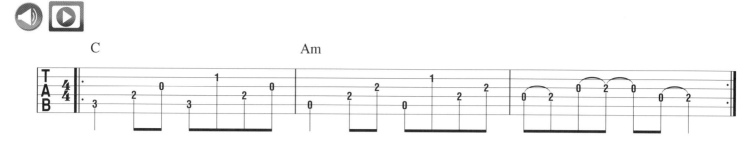

SLIDE FILLS

A slide can be played in a variety of different ways, all of which can work wonderfully as a fill. Often the tricky bit is working out which finger to start on. In this example, try fretting the first note of the phrase with your third finger. This gets you ready to slide up to fret 4 and in position to play fret 3 on the B string with your second finger. In the second measure, also use your third finger to hammer-on to fret 2 on the D string. This will set you up nicely for the E chord.

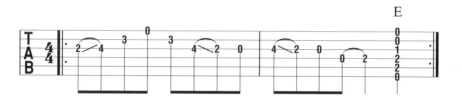

James Taylor is one of the world's most renowned fingerpickers, and in this classic track, "Fire and Rain," we can hear why. The ornamentation between notes is tricky to play but an absolute joy to hear. The chords above the music are there to show harmonic movement. It's not necessary at this time to learn completely new chord shapes to play through the tune.

"Fire and Rain"

John Mayer has a unique fingerpicking style and is a fan of fingerstyle fills. His track, "Stop This Train," is a fabulous example of how a constant pattern can be refreshingly reframed with the simplest of fills. Notice the hammer-on in the first bar, the slides between the bars, and the string slap notated with an "X." Again, don't worry about the unfamiliar chord names above the music. They are there for reference to show the harmonic structure.

"Stop This Train"

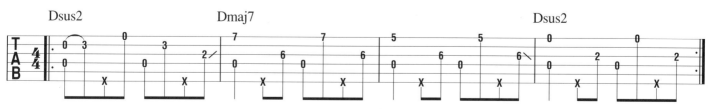

This tune is a staple of the fingerpicking diet. It uses a constant thumb-and-fingers combination (Travis-picking style), which is worth getting confident with. The tune is almost entirely based around an A minor shape, so the little finger on the fret hand does a lot of the work to reach other notes. Once you're confident with the pattern in the first bar, your next real challenge is between bars 5 and 6. Here your little finger will slide down from fret 4 to fret 3 as the hand returns to a familiar A minor shape—it is the main feature of the piece.

"Windy and Warm"

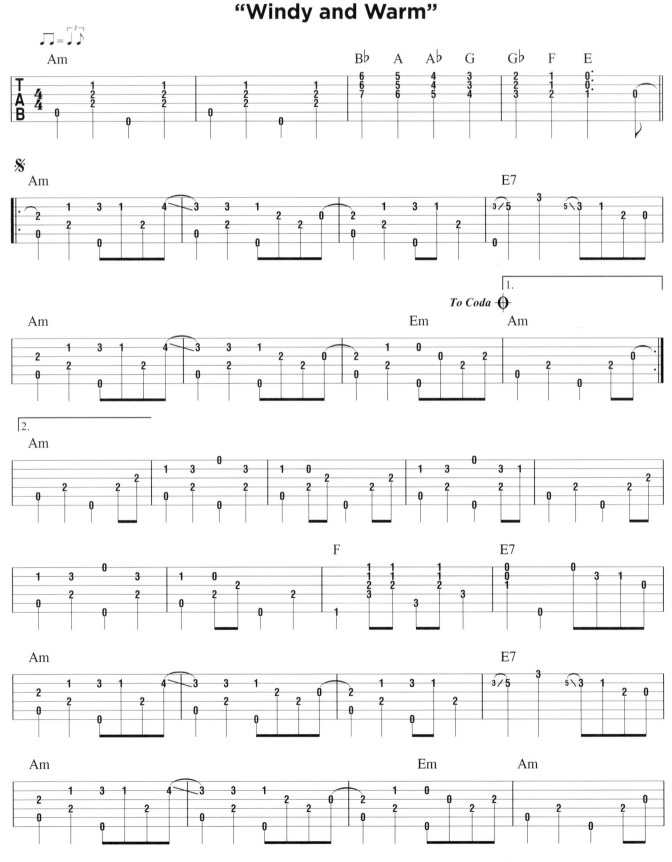

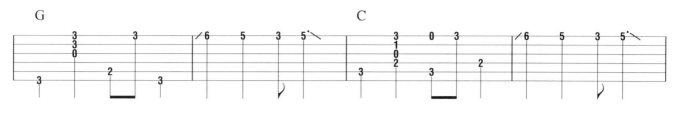

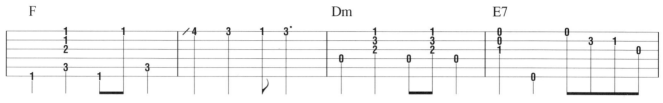

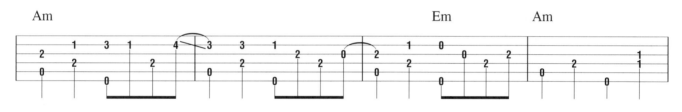

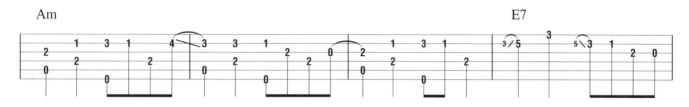

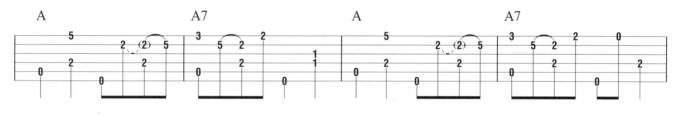

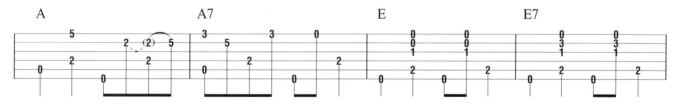

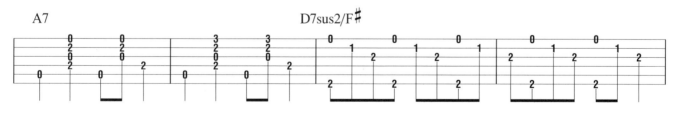

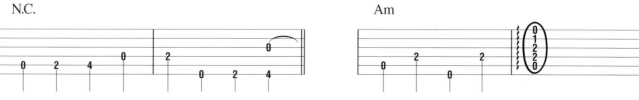

D.S. al Coda   ⊕ **Coda**

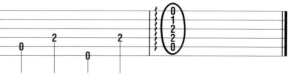

ABOUT THE AUTHOR

Chris Woods is a UK-based guitarist, composer, and educator. Recording as "The Chris Woods Groove Orchestra," he is renowned as an explorer of the guitar, always pushing the boundaries of the instrument. A fingerstyle virtuoso with a love for inspiring others.

www.chriswoodsgroove.co.uk